T _d & tested tips & techniques
from school librarians

editor Claire Larson

www.carelpress.com
www.strictlylibrary.com

CAREL PRESS

Contents

(Pages in brackets refer to copiable worksheets)

© 2008 Carel Press & Individual contributors
Editor & designer: Claire Larson
Advisers: Christine A Shepherd, Chas White
Readers: Inga Bozier, Pat Chandler, Jennifer Toerien,
Carol Williams
Cover design: Jack Croal
Published by Carel Press Ltd
4 Hewson St
Carlisle CA2 5AU
Tel + 44 1228 538928
Fax + 44 1228 591816
info@carelpress.com
www.carelpress.com
www.StrictlyLibrary.com

Reproduction from this resource is allowed only within
the individual purchasing institution.
Printed by: Finemark, Poland
CIP Data: British Library Cataloguing in Publication
Data is available
ISBN: 978 1 905600 12 0

Contents - by type of activity

Some projects appear in more than one category
(Pages in brackets refer to copiable worksheets)

Introduction

School librarians are immensely creative, coming up with inspired ways to promote their libraries, attract students and staff and support students in their learning. **Great Library Ideas** came about from a desire to share these bright ideas, fabulous projects and successful strategies. It's easy to share ideas with one or two colleagues, but often that's as far as it goes. **Great Library Ideas** takes it that step further, presenting suggestions sent in by librarians from across the country and sharing this good practice with as many people as possible.

Whether you are looking for a long term project to promote reading or an emergency fill in for an unexpected lesson, **Great Library Ideas** can help. Fun quizzes and competitions, strategies to raise the profile of the library, ways to help students get to know their library, and suggestions for teaching information skills are all included, complete with librarians' notes and worksheets.

Each idea offers full instructions, suggestions on how to take it further and references to other similar themes covered by **Great Library Ideas**.

Claire Larson

Networking without Wires!

There is much that a school librarian can learn from modern management theory in the field of social networks. *The Strength of Weak Ties* is a famous paper by sociologist Mark Granovetter and it can be successfully applied to the school librarian. We all have lots of strong ties: family and close friends and work colleagues, but we should also cultivate weak ties which are the contacts with people outside our immediate circle, for example the teachers in a school.

Granovetter found that people who developed and maintained their weak ties were enriched personally and in their job. They had a wide range of contacts informally feeding them information. This develops a real feeling of social cohesion, and if an individual needs support or advice, they can quickly and effectively receive it. As the post of school librarian can be an isolated one, this is especially important.

Weak ties, or effective networking, are absolutely central to the role of the school librarian. We all know that cataloguing, classification and so on are important, but these are the visible externals of a library. For users to benefit they have to come through the door.

A school library is only at the heart of a school's learning when the librarian is in contact with the widest possible range of teachers and students. The passive librarian waits for users to come to the library. The active librarian goes out to meet staff from all departments, not just those that are traditionally linked with the library such as English. Of course, every librarian will have particular teachers that they get on well with and that they enjoy talking to, but the effective librarian makes a point of reaching out to all staff.

This may not come naturally to all, but it pays enormous dividends. The librarian will be in touch with what is happening throughout the school and how the library could better meet staff and student needs. New users can be encouraged, new contacts forged, new ideas sparked.

Unfortunately in some schools the library is little used by some members of staff. This is revealed in a number of ways, for example at exhibitions when a teacher and a librarian are visiting exhibitor stands together, a teacher will sometimes exclaim 'If only we had this resource in our school', for the librarian then to say 'but we have it, didn't you know?'

Effective networking takes effort and organisation. Many people might prefer to talk just to those colleagues they already know. The networking librarian reaches out. Why not:
• Make a new contact every day
• Talk to someone you don't know in the staffroom or at school social events
• Host meetings to welcome new members of staff
• Attend various department meetings
• Get involved in something not connected with the library

There are all sorts of approaches you could try, for example take a new resource to a department or particular teacher. Everyone appreciates personal service!

The most important type of networking for librarians involves neither wires nor any expense. Remember that the best librarian is 'a snapper-up of unconsidered trifles' (Shakespeare, *A Winter's Tale*) – and it's by networking that you'll find these.

In essence every school librarian can become a broker of knowledge, someone who, through developing these weak ties, becomes aware of knowledge and information resources in one part of the school that are precisely what is needed in another part of the school. In this way, the librarian provides not just resources from her or his own library stock but also is able to act as a kind of centre for knowledge transmission. In the jargon of modern management theory this is known as spanning across structural holes!

Many of the activities in Great Library Ideas will help you do this – so try these ideas and start spanning!

Chas White: ideas developed from discussions with Martin Kilduff, Professor of Management, University of Texas at Austin.
The Strength of Weak Ties, American Journal of Sociology, 1973

Mystery Gift

by Nikki Heath

Type of activity

Promoting Reading

Suggested time

Librarian's time approx 2 hours

How it works

This is an event you can plan for a holiday such as Christmas or the summer break. It goes down really well in my school, although it does take a bit of time to prepare. We wrap up new fiction and non fiction stock as presents, put the date due and barcode number on a gift tag and attach the tags to the books.

The week before we break up we display all the wrapped 'presents' so that they look enticing - we might arrange them around a Christmas tree, or pile them up next to a deck chair. Students are then encouraged to borrow a mystery book. The idea is that it will extend their reading as they may end up with a book they would not usually have considered.

Taking it further

Ask students to submit book reviews and award something appropriately seasonal (selection boxes, Easter eggs etc) to the top ten.

Have genre book lists available so that if a student did read and enjoy a book from a genre they haven't tried before you can be on hand to recommend other titles in the same genre.

Target met?

Encourages students to read more widely and to try books by authors and genres they may not have previously considered.

See also

Desert Island Books

Book Walls

Book Menus

Speed Dating

Blind Date

Send a Text Message to a Book Character

Around the World in Fiction

Best Borrowers

by Fay Nelmes

Type of activity

Raising the profile of the Library

Suggested time

Librarian's time, approx one hour

How it works

Why not make use of your library system to reward consistently high borrowing levels? You should be able to obtain an accurate picture of how many books are being borrowed and who is borrowing the most. In my school the top male and female borrower in each key stage is rewarded each term with a book token and certificate.

You have to keep tabs on anyone borrowing vast amounts just so they can win, but it's quite apparent who is borrowing for genuine purposes and it's nice to reward the unsung heroes who just get on with school life and make use of the library, borrowing regularly to help with homework and to read for pleasure.

Target met?

Recognises library use and rewards reading achievement.

See also

Murder in the Library

Guess Who's Coming to Dinner

Loyalty Card Scheme

Create a Learning Climate

Taking it further

There is always the possibility of using the statistics offered by your library system to monitor which form group is using the library most and returning their books on time! Rewards for the best form could comprise merits or house points. Anything to keep the library in the forefront of students' minds, and get them borrowing and returning books regularly.

Book Menus

by Sonia Constantinou

Type of activity

Promoting Reading

Suggested time

One lesson

How it works

The book menu was a World Book Day event that tied in with the theme of food. Students were given copies of a blank menu and had to put down:

- a starter: something small and appetising
- a main course: a satisfying read and
- a dessert: something delicious and fun

Taking it further

Menus could be displayed around the school. From the menus it should be possible to build book lists of recommended 'dishes' or reads that could be used for further promotion and display.

Target met?

Encourages students to talk about what they have read and to demonstrate how different books can be fulfilling in different ways.

See also

Desert Island Books

Book Walls

Mystery Gift

Speed Dating

Blind Date

Send a Text Message...

Around the World in Fiction

Worksheet

on page 41

Desert Island Books

by Polly Mortimer

Type of activity

Promoting Reading

Suggested time

One lesson or students' free time

How it works

This is run along the same lines as the radio programme. Ask students to vote for a number of books (you decide how many, but four to six works best) that they couldn't live without if they were stranded on a desert island. Following this they have to pick the one book that is their absolute favourite above all the others.

Count up the votes and see which books prove to be the most popular.

Taking it further

Involve the teachers (especially popular ones) in voting for their favourite books and possibly get the students to contact their favourite author or any other well known people to find out their desert island books too. This could be an interesting activity for your reading group.

Set a challenge to persuade students to read the top book from their friend's or teacher's top desert island books.

This activity offers plenty of scope for display and should encourage wider reading.

Target met?

Encourages students to read more widely and to try books by authors and genres they may not have previously considered.

See also

Book Menus

Book Walls

Mystery Gift

Speed Dating

Blind Date Reads

Send a Text Message...

Around the World in Fiction

Worksheet on page 42

Desert Island Books!

You are about to be shipwrecked on a desert island. Fortunately the ship you are on has a huge library containing almost every book ever published, so at least you won't be short of things to read!

Your task is to decide on the four books you would most like to have with you on your desert island.

1 ....
2 ....
3 ....
4 ....

Finally, from the four listed above, which is your absolute favourite book?

The one book I must have is:

Book Walls

by Polly Mortimer

Type of activity

Promoting Reading

Suggested time

Students to complete in free time or during one lesson

How it works

Create a book wall. This can be done quickly and easily. Back a display board with light coloured paper. Create the wall effect by cutting a square of sponge and dipping it in dark red paint or ink and stamping the wall at regular intervals to create the effect of bricks.

Students jot down their favourite books on post it notes and these are added to the wall.

Target met?

Encourages students to talk about what they have read and to recommend books to others.

See also

Desert Island Books

Mystery Gift

Speed Dating

Blind Date Reads

Book Menus

Send a Text Message to a Book Character

Taking it further

Arrange the suggestions by genres on the wall and use them to create genre based bookmarks with suggested titles.

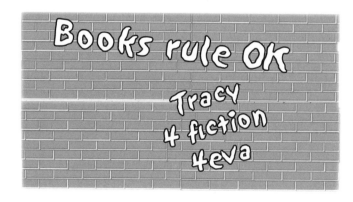

Send a Text Message to a Book Character
by Nikki Heath

Type of activity

Promoting Reading and Quiz/Competition

How it works

Get your students to choose a character from any book and write him or her a text message.

Taking it further

This could be run as a competition, with prizes for the most ingenious and original messages. Text messages submitted could be displayed next to the book to promote it to other readers. Remind your students that these are 'hooks' to encourage students to read the book, so they must make sure their text message doesn't give too much of the plot away!

Suggested time

One lesson
or complete as competition during free time

Target met?

Encourages students to think about what they have read and to empathise with characters in their favourite books.

See also

Desert Island Books

Book Walls

Mystery Gift

Speed Dating

Blind Date Reads

Book Menus

Worksheets

on pages 43 & 44

Book Ends Quiz - Match the Book and Film Pairs

by Nikki Heath

Type of activity

Quiz/Competition

How it works

This activity could be run to tie in with Valentine's Day. Each question asks you to match the book and film couples.

Taking it further

Run as a competition and offer prizes.

Target met?

Fun activity.

See also

Guess the Genre

Guess Who's Coming to Dinner

Murder in the Library

Send a Text Message...

Worksheet

on page 45

Suggested time

Students' free time as a competition

Quiz answers

1 Hermione Granger & Victor Krum
2 Artemis Fowl & Holly Short
3 Gollum & The Ring
4 Willy Wonka & Charlie Bucket
5 Luke Skywalker & Darth Vader
6 Bridget Jones & Mark Darcy
7 Beauty and the Beast
8 Count Olaf & the Beaudelaire Children
9 Romeo & Juliet

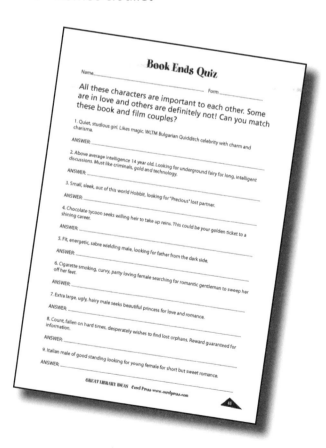

Non Fiction Detective
by Nikki Heath

Type of activity

Getting to Know the Library

Suggested time

One lesson

How it works

A two part quiz. Part 1 gives students practice in using the subject index and/or library catalogue to find the Dewey numbers for certain subjects. Part 2 gives them the Dewey numbers and asks them to find the correct section in the library and to identify the overall subject.

See also:

The Dewey Game

Library Treasure Hunt Bingo

Murder in the Library

Lateral Thinking Game

Transition Project

Target met?

Helps students familiarise themselves with the Dewey Decimal system and offers practice in finding books and identifying different subject areas.

Worksheet:

on page 46

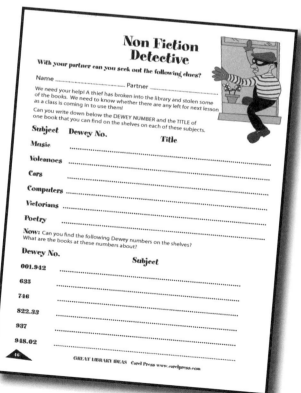

Guess the Genre

by Nikki Heath

Type of activity

Quiz/Competition

How it works

A quiz to test your students' knowledge of opening lines. They have to decide which genre the books belong to.

Target met?

Fun activity

See also

Book Ends
Guess Who's Coming to Dinner
Send a Text Message
Murder in the Library

Worksheet

on page 47

Suggested time

Students' free time as a competition

Answers to quiz

1 Humour (Sachar, L *Dogs Don't Tell Jokes*)
2 Mystery (Sachar, L *Holes*)
3 Fantasy (Tolkien, J R R *The Hobbit*)
4 Crime (Horowitz, A *Scorpia*)
5 Animals (Burgess, M *Tiger Tiger*)
6 Sport (Peet, M *Keeper*)
7 Adventure (Korman, G *Everest*)
8 Mystery (Snicket, L *The Bad Beginning*)

Guess the Genre

Can you guess which genre these opening lines are from? (The genres are all at the bottom of this page...)

1) This story begins with a smile... ....

2) There is no lake at Camp Green Lake ....

3) In a hole in the ground their lived a Hobbit ....

4) For the two thieves of the 200cc scooter, it was a case of the wrong victim, in the wrong place, on the wrong Sunday morning in September.
....

5) The sheep were released at the Eastern end of the killing pen.
....

6) Paul Faustino slid a blank into the tape recorder and stabbed a couple of buttons.
....

7) It was a funeral in every way but one: the body was missing
....

8) If you are interested in stories with a happy ending, you would be better off reading some other book.
....

Mystery	Animals	Sports	Sci-Fi
Fantasy	Adventure	Horror	Crime
Suspense	Humour		

Find a Fact
by Nikki Heath

Type of activity

Information Skills

Suggested time

Part of one lesson
or students' free time

How it works

A quick activity to get students using encyclopaedias and sifting through information to find something that interests them. A purposeful 'fill in' or fun activity.

See also

The Shakespeare Reading Game

Web versus Books

Lateral Thinking Game

Target met?

Purposeful 'fill in' or fun activity to develop skills in using multi volume encyclopaedias

Worksheet

on page 48

Find a Fact

Name: .... Form: ....

This is a fun lesson for you. Here's what you have to do:

FIND the multi-volumed reference encyclopaedias

FIND the volume of the Encyclopaedia that begins with the first letter of your surname. (Be very careful here as some of the volumes finish or start with half a letter, for example A-Ch, Ci - G).

LIST anything in that volume that interests you:

....
....
....
....

READ through the information and
FIND the most amazing fact or sentence you can:

....
....

WRITE it into your own words:

....
....
....
....

and then **ILLUSTRATE** it

When you have finished put the encyclopaedia volume back in the correct place.   Tick when returned ☑

48

GREAT LIBRARY IDEAS   Carel Press www.carelpress.com

The Shakespeare Reading Game
by Bev Stuttard

Type of activity

Information Skills

Suggested time

One or two lessons

How it works

This project runs along similar lines to Carel's very popular Reading Game where students view and evaluate books from a variety of genres. For this game different aspects of Shakespeare's life and work are researched including theatre, biography, plays and trivia.

Appropriate information and a series of questions are placed on each table around the library. Students then spend ten to fifteen minutes on each topic before moving on to the next one. We used this as an introduction to Shakespeare for 13 to 14 year olds. It proved popular with the students, and teachers were impressed at how focused and on task the students were.

See also

Find a Fact

Web versus Books

Lateral Thinking Game

Worksheets

on pages 49 to 52

Target met?

Introduces students to Shakespeare and provides practice in searching for and recording information.

Shakespeare's Plays

You will find examples of Shakespeare's plays. Can you divide them up into History, Tragedy, Comedy.

History:

Tragedy:

Comedy:

Choose one play in each group and write down the

Title

Where it is set

Two of the main characters

The year it was probably written

Title

Where it is set

Two of the main characters

The year it was probably written

Title

Where it is set

Two of the main characters

Shakespeare's The

The first theatre in London was built in 1567, what was it

In 1603 Shakespeare's theatre company changed its name
M Why?
The Globe Theatre was not round. Can you find out how

Where abouts in London was the Globe Theatre?
How many people could watch plays in the Globe?
Why were some spectators called groundlings?

How much did it cost to watch a play as a groundling?
If you wanted a seat, how much would it cost?
What year did The Globe burn down?
Which Shakespeare play was being performed at the time

Shakespeare in Stra

Shakespeare was born on the
of His father was call
and his mother
living as a
school when he was years old. He went
school where the main subjects he learned were
in 1582 he married
They had
After many years in London Shakespeare returned to Stra
bought a large house called
died on
ied in aged church in Strat
most of his property to his daughter
daughter Judith received and his w

Shakespeare's Theatre - Answers

The first theatre in London was built in 1567, what was it called? *The Theatre*

In 1603 Shakespeare's theatre company changed its name to the *King's Men. Because James 1st had become king after the death of Elizabeth 1st*

The Globe Theatre was not round. Can you find out how many sides it had? *It had 20 sides*

Whereabouts in London was the Globe Theatre? *Bankside*

How many people could watch plays in the Globe? *3,000*

Why were some spectators called groundlings? *Because they would stand to watch the play*

How much did it cost to watch a play as a groundling? *One old penny to stand in the yard*

If you wanted a seat, how much would it cost? *A cushioned seat in the gallery cost three old pennies*

What year did The Globe burn down? *1613*

Which Shakespeare play was being performed at the time? *Henry VIII*

Shakespeare in Stratford - Answers

Shakespeare was born on the ***23rd April 1564*** in the town of ***Stratford-Upon-Avon.*** His father was called ***John*** and his mother ***Mary Arden.*** His father made his living as a ***glove maker.*** William probably started school when he was ***six*** years old. He went to the local grammar school where the main subjects he learned were ***Latin*** and ***Greek.*** In 1582 he married ***Anne Hathaway.*** They had ***three*** children.

After many years in London Shakespeare returned to Stratford to retire. He bought a large house called ***New Place.*** He died on ***23rd April 1616*** aged ***52 years*** and was buried in ***Holy Trinity*** church in Stratford. In his will he left most of his property to his daughter ***Susanna***, but his other daughter Judith received ***£300*** and his wife ***the second best bed***

Shakespeare in London - Answers

When did Shakespeare probably go to London? *During the 1580s*

Which group of actors did he join? *He joined the Lord Chamberlain's Men*

Can you find the name of three theatres in London at the time. *The Swan, The Rose, The Theatre or The Curtain*

Why did all the theatres have to close down in 1592? *Because of an outbreak of plague*

When did the theatres reopen? *in 1594*

How many people lived in London at that time? *200,000*

Shakespeare worked with many famous actors, can you find the names of three of them? *Will Sly, Will Kemp, Richard Burbage or Edward Alleyn*

Shakespeare's England - Answers

Who was queen of England when Shakespeare was born? *Elizabeth 1st*

During the 1580s England was at war with France or Spain *(Circle the correct answer)* *Spain*

A large fleet of ships sent to invade England was defeated in 1588. It was called the *Spanish Armada*

What was the name of the famous English explorer who sailed around the world at this time? *Sir Francis Drake*

Most people lived in the town or the country? (Circle the correct word). *Country*

Can you write down the names of five things people did for entertainment. *Hawking, hunting, board games, archery, football, cockfighting, bear baiting, visiting theatres, attending executions.*

How did people travel in Shakespeare's time? *The poor walked. Richer people had horses and some had carriages.*

Twelfth Night - Answers

Twelfth Night is one of Shakespeare's *comedy* plays. It takes place in the country of *Illyria* and the ruler, or Duke, is called *Orsino*. The Duke is in love with a lady called *Olivia* who is not in love with him.

A young girl called *Viola* believes she is the only survivor of a shipwreck and disguises herself as a *boy* so she can become a page to the Duke. She calls herself *Cesario*. She looks very like her brother *Sebastian* who is believed lost in the shipwreck. There are lots of parts in Shakespeare's plays where girls are disguised as boys, but female roles were always played by *boy* actors.

The Duke uses his page to send messages to Olivia to try to persuade her to love him. Viola is sad because she has fallen in love with the Duke.

Living in Olivia's house is her cousin Sir *Toby Belch*, a clown called *Feste,* her steward *Malvolio* and her servant girl *Maria*. The others all play a trick on the steward and persuade him that Olivia loves him. He finds a letter which he is convinced is from Olivia. It tells him to wear *yellow cross garters*. Olivia is shocked and convinced Malvolio is mad. Viola's brother *Sebastian* is discovered to be alive and Olivia, who has fallen in love with the Duke's page, transfers her love to him. The Duke, who is confused by his feelings for his page, is delighted to discover she is a girl and marries her.

Everyday Phrases - Answers

Which plays do the following come from?

The be all and end all - *Macbeth*

A blinking idiot - *Merchant of Venice*

Neither rhyme nor reason - *As You Like It*

Cruel to be kind - *Hamlet*

He hath eaten me out of house and home - *Henry IV Part Two*

All that glitters is not gold - *Merchant of Venice*

Too much of a good thing - *As You Like It.*

The Dewey Game
by Sue Bastone & Roz Heinze

Type of activity

Getting to Know the Library

How it works

This activity is aimed at pupils new to middle/high school.

You will need to make A3 size mats for each Dewey 100. I made them by creating a collage of pictures to represent the subjects in each of the 100 categories, for example 200s religions, 700s arts etc. These were then laminated so they could be used over and over again. Six different mats should be enough for a class to use. Before the students come into the library the mats are placed on the floor near the appropriate Dewey section. Underneath each mat are copies of the relevant worksheet (see pages 53 - 57). Also on the mat are a ruler and a pencil.

When the students come in the first thing they are asked to do is remove their shoes - this always causes a bit of excitement and starts the session off in a relaxed fashion. They are then asked to get themselves into groups of five or six (depending on the class size), give themselves a group name and go to the nearest mat.

Each group will be asked to pick up one worksheet from under their mat. The librarian then explains the game by saying that they will be given a maximum of ten minutes to complete their worksheet. If they finish before that time they must return to their mat, every group member must have one foot on the mat and put a hand up. At the end of the first ten minute session a whistle is blown (optional depending on whether you have other students studying in the library, but great fun!) Their group name is written at the top of the sheet and handed in. Each group then moves round to the next mat (clockwise or anti-clockwise) and waits for the starter whistle.

Suggested time

One lesson

Each worksheet has the same questions at the beginning and end and different ones in the middle. Each session tends to get quicker with great competition to be the first group to finish.

Although this game can be a bit chaotic, we found that it really did help with the familiarisation process of where each section was, roughly what was in it and how the Dewey Decimal system is organised.

Target met?

An introduction to the Dewey system.

See also

The Non Fiction Detective.

Library Treasure Hunt Bingo

Murder in the Library

The Lateral Thinking Game

Dewey Jumble Sale

Worksheets on pages 53 to 57

Mission Possible
by Julie Glasel

Type of activity

Promoting Reading

How it works

Mission Possible is a series of reading missions for students to complete. The aim is to challenge them to widen their reading choices. While they are reading they will also earn bronze, silver and gold awards.

To earn a bronze award a student must complete seven missions (read six books) the first six missions can be completed in any order. The seventh mission is to prepare a talk on the book or story they enjoyed the most.

A silver award is obtained by following the same missions but choosing a different selection of books.

The gold award can be won by completing a further seven missions from Mission Possible, Going for Gold (see page 64)

There is no time limit. Obviously the books selected must complement your own library stock. Students can be encouraged to choose a different book from your own list that would fit the same genre, providing they check with you or their English teacher first.

We made Mission Possible booklets available either through the library or the English Department. We also promoted the scheme in assemblies, via the school bulletin and, of course, in the library. We chose to award medals as we are a Sports College. A roll of students gaining each award could be displayed in the library.

Suggested time

Introduction during one lesson
Completed during students' free time

Target met?

The OFSTED self evaluation criteria for secondary school libraries requires students to access challenging reading materials. This goes some way towards promoting that.

See also

Read a Rainbow

Book Menus

Desert Island Books

Speed Dating

Blind Date Reads

Worksheets   on pages 58 to 64

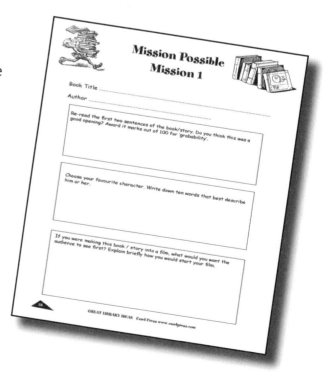

Murder in the Library
by Alison Squibb

Type of activity

Raising Library Profile *and*
Getting to Know the Library *and* Quiz

How it works

The idea of Murder in the Library is to encourage students into the library to use and develop their library skills. We usually run it as a competition at break and lunch times over a period of three to four weeks.

Initially the event is advertised with lots of inviting and eye-catching posters along the lines: 'A Murder is About to Happen!' and 'It's Murder in the Library!' (see pages 65 to 66). Clues are then offered which have to be solved using various library skills (samples of these are on page 67). The clues can be adapted to suit different levels of ability. Puzzles can be added, or cryptic clues used, depending on the skills you want highlighted.

Our experience is that students get very involved, especially if a teacher is the murderer! They love any gory details that can be added and appreciate the use of blood stains (red ink), fingerprints (in black or red ink) and the use of authentic 'Police Do Not Cross' tape, which our local police station was happy to provide.

The students are so enthused that they use their library skills without realising it when solving clues. It's also a great way to encourage reluctant students into the library.

See page 22 for a timetable and explanation of Murder in the Library

See pages 65 to 66 for suggested posters to advertise the event.

See page 67 for sample questions. You would have to create your own to fit the names of your victim and murderer!

Suggested time

Students' free time

Target met?

Helps students develop their skills in finding and using information. Also helps to familiarise them with the layout of the library and what's on offer.

See also

Send a Text Message...

Library Treasure Hunt Bingo

Best Borrowers

The Lateral Thinking Game

Guess Who's Coming to Dinner

Worksheets

on pages 65 to 67

A Murder is about to happen in the library
Are you a good enough detective to solve the mystery?

Visit the library on

....

And prepare to be SHOCKED!

Librarian's Notes
Timetable and Explanation for Murder in the Library

Week before Murder in Library Event
Put posters around the school advertising:
'It's Murder in Our Library' 'Murder Most Foul'
'A Murder is About to Happen'.

Use bright colours. Make 'bloody' fingerprints on posters with red ink. Let students know by announcing in registration that a murder is about to happen in the library.

Week 1 of Murder in the Library
Make a body outline on the floor in the library by using masking tape. Use 'Police do not Cross' tape to seal off the area and indicate the crime scene.

Put a pile of clue sheets out on the library counter.

First set of clues will lead to the name of the victim. (Re-arrange first letter of each answer to reveal victim - a member of the teaching staff).

This set of clues will run for one week.

Week 2
Second set of clues available in the library.

Lay out some clues next to the body outline (ie a piece of rope, a bottle marked poison and a toy gun etc).

Second set of clues will lead to the way that the victim was murdered. Rearrange first letter of each answer to reveal how the murder was committed.

This set of clues will be available for one week.

Week 3
Third and final set of clues available in the library.

Third set of clues will lead to the identity of the murderer (Re-arrange first letter of each answer to reveal who the murderer was - a member of the teaching staff.)

This set of clues will be available for one week.

Closing Date.
Choose a closing date for all entries to the murder quiz.

Only accept fully completed entries (all questions have to be answered correctly, not just the name of the victim put forward etc).

Prizes awarded to winners during assemblies.

Answers to all the clues, with names of winners are posted up in the library after the event.

NB Clues can be set according to ability of students.

Make sure that permission is secured from members of staff who will be victim and murderer.

Swear members of staff to secrecy as some students will ask if they are the victim or murderer.

GREAT LIBRARY IDEAS Carel Press www.carelpress.com

Guess Who's Coming to Dinner
by Anita Barry

Type of activity

Quiz/Competition
and Raising the Profile of the Library

How it works

Lots of books or characters are associated with food, so I simply laid a small table and put a few clues for each character and labelled it as 'Guess who's coming to dinner.'

The hardest part is collecting all the props! It looks very eye-catching when set up and students really enjoy guessing the characters. See page 68 for suggestions on characters and food.

Taking it further

Following on from this came 'Shhh....who's been reading here?' which works in a similar way but incorporates library books into the display. We set up a different book corner each week over a number of weeks, which kept the students' interest and meant they had to come in each week to guess the character.

I ran 'Guess who's coming to dinner' and 'Shhh...who's been reading here' at different times as competitions. They could be adapted as a flat display using pictures of items rather than actual objects, or set up in a corner of the library for an open evening or parent evening.

Suggested time

Students' free time

Target met?

A fun activity to promote and raise the profile of the library.

See also

Book Ends

Guess the Genre

Send a Text Message

Murder in the Library

Best Borrowers

Loyalty Card Scheme

Worksheet

on page 68

Library Treasure Hunt Bingo

by Duncan Wright

Type of activity

Getting to Know the Library

Suggested time

One lesson

How it works

Students are split into teams of up to six people in each team. It is essential to have the same number of people in each team. Members of each team are allocated a number between one and six. Each member of the team must have a different number. Students should write their number on a sticker and stick it to their shirt so it is clearly visible to everyone.

The object of the game is to collect various items from around the library. See page 69.

The Bingo Caller calls out a number. The students with that number must go and collect one of the items on the list. The items can be collected in any order.

Only one member of the group may be away at any time. Nobody else may leave the group until the previous member of the team has returned, even if another group member's number has been called.

The first group to collect all the items on the list must shout BINGO to be declared the winner.

Taking it further

This game could be adapted for students to gain practice in finding books by specific authors, different genres, or even non fiction topics.

Target met?

Helps students to become familiar with the layout of the library and demonstrates some of the resources available.

See also

The Dewey Game

The Non Fiction Detective

Murder in the Library

The Lateral Thinking Game

Dewey Jumble Sale

Worksheet

on page 69

Library Treasure Hunt Bingo
Suggested Resources to be Found

- A fiction book
- Today's Newspapers
- A book about your local area
- An encyclopaedia
- An audio book
- A reference book
- A non fiction book
- Something from your teacher
- A magazine
- A poetry book

What do we read?

by Claire Harrison

Type of activity

Promoting Reading

Suggested time

One lesson

How it works

This came about when I asked a Year 7 group to tell me who thought of themselves as 'a reader'. Very few did, even those who had been borrowing from the library regularly. I targeted these pupils initially, asking why they hadn't put their hand up, to be told it was because they read non fiction. I then asked who thought a reader was someone who read fiction. Most of the class raised their hands.

We spent the next quarter of an hour trying to think of things you read other than fiction. Once I'd done this with all my Year 7 groups I made a large display: 'What Year 7 Read', where we had all their responses printed out in different sizes and fonts. The total came to 153 and included things as diverse as menus, logos, tree rings, badges, calculators, lips and text messages. Once they realised that no comment was too outrageous, providing it was true, they became very keen to contribute.

The display was mounted in the library and brought lots of interested people in to look, and some were prompted to add their own ideas. For me it was an opportunity to highlight reading as the everyday necessity it is. We decided to add our heading: 'Everyone needs to read, every day!'

Target met?

Raises awareness that we all need to read and encourages students to think of themselves as readers.

See also

Book Walls

Book Menus

Desert Island Books

Take a Book by its Cover

Speed Dating

Blind Date Reads

Web versus Books

by Fay Nelmes

Type of activity

Information Skills

Suggested time

One lesson

How it works

This is a useful activity for older students as it gets them thinking about different sources of information and helps them to make informed decisions about choosing the most appropriate information source.

Students are given a series of ten research scenarios. For each they need to decide whether it would be quicker, easier and more relevant to use a book to find the information or the internet. Initially they jot down their ideas as to which information source would be best - book or internet. Following this they have a go at finding the information required and jot down how they went about their search, what worked and what didn't. For this exercise the answer is less important than the method they used to get there. They report back and discuss their findings with the rest of the class.

Taking it further

There are endless possibilities to this activity. Is it quicker to find out what's on at the cinema by checking the internet or the local newspaper? A stop-watch can add to the fun here! How do we know whether a website is more accurate than a book? Students enjoy the challenge of comparing the internet and print resources to find specific information, and it's a useful way of getting across some of the issues of internet usage.

Target met?

Raises important issues about sources of information and how to use them.

See also

The Lateral Thinking Game

Find a Fact

Shakespeare Reading Game

Worksheet

on page 70

The Web versus Books

Finding the Information
For this activity you will need to work in pairs. Here are a series of seven research scenarios. For each one you need to decide whether it will be quicker, easier and more relevant to use a book to find the information, or the internet.

To start with just read each research scenario and jot down next to it which source of information you think will be best. Then have a go at the research and make notes about how easy it was to find the information using your chosen source. Make sure you quote each source. Later on we will discuss your findings with the rest of the class.

Research Scenrio:	Book or Internet?	Notes about Research (including Source)
What are the Opening hours of the Colisseum in Rome?		
In what city would you find the famous Rialto Bridge?		
Which city is further south, Naples or Milan?		
What are the two large islands of the coast of Italy?		
What year was Pompeii destroyed by Mount Vesuvius?		
Are there any rules to follow when visiting the Vatican?		
How much is a train ticket from Ciampinon Airport to Roma Termini?		

Take a Book by its Cover

by Linda Bromyard

Type of activity

Promoting Reading

Suggested time

One lesson

How it works

This project aims to encourage pupils to think about the importance of book covers in helping us to decide what to read. To make the lesson enjoyable and a bit different I use sweets as an example. I get them to look at a variety of sweet packets and ask them to think about various aspects of their design and what makes a sweet package look attractive. We then hold the same discussion but link it to book covers instead. I find this activity gets the students thinking and talking about their own preferences and how important a book cover is in encouraging them to choose that particular book.

Taking it further

This lesson is a useful launch pad for a further lesson discussing how we go about choosing the book we want to read and taking into account blurbs, recommendations, genres, advertising etc.

Target met?

Encourages students to talk about what they have read and to think about the importance of book covers in influencing their choice of book.

See also

Desert Island Books

Book Walls

Book Menus

Worksheet

on page 71

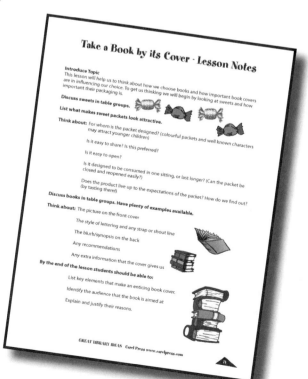

The Lateral Thinking Game

by Sarah Pavey

Type of activity

Getting to Know the Library *and* Information Skills

How it works

This project came about when I started thinking about the kinds of information that students were looking for. I noticed that younger pupils (aged 13 - 16) tended to ask for factual information that was fairly easy to locate on the catalogue or the internet, whereas sixth form students were often given conceptual information to find.

I designed an answer sheet for pupils (see pages 73 & 74) which has a list of all the shelf headings in the library. At the top of the sheet is written the name of a topic that students will research. You need to come up with a series of suitable topics; they could be factual topics such as animals, transport, diseases or conceptual ones such as poverty, diversity, wealth or vanity.

Students work in pairs to research their topic. For each shelf heading they have to find a resource that in some way connects to the word they have been given. The link can be very tenuous and it is up to them to find it. For example, if they are researching the topic 'animals' they may pick a book that has a picture of an animal on the front cover, it might be that the author's name is Mr Rabbit, it might be because the publisher is Lion, or it might be because the title gives us a clue, for example 'Too Much to Bear' would be acceptable and underpins the lateral thinking element of the project! For each resource found, students make a note of the connection point to their research topic, the title and the Dewey number.

Pupils work in pairs or threes and this helps to generate discussion and creativity. I encourage everyone to start with what they think will be the easiest shelf heading for their topic. I also encourage them to ask the library staff lots of questions and to share the information they have found. I collect the sheets and reward the best and most original entry with chocolate and a certificate.

I have found that this activity keeps students on task and increases their awareness of what is in the library because the emphasis is on finding and looking at resources and making decisions about them.

Suggested time

One lesson

At the end of the lesson I try to have a brief discussion about how difficult they found the activity. What was the easiest resource to find, the most difficult resource and the answer that they felt most satisfied with. I then emphasise that lateral thinking is a very useful quality when it comes to coursework and exams.

Target met?

Increases awareness of what is in the library and helps students understand that information for a topic is rarely found in only one place. Allows students to decide for themselves which resources are most appropriate.

See also

Non Fiction Detective

Dewey Game

Library Treasure Hunt Bingo

Murder in the Library

Worksheets on pages 72 to 74

Read a Rainbow

by Helen Hinks

Type of activity

Promoting Reading

How it works

This came about when I thought how often we use colour to describe our mood - whether we are tickled pink or browned off! I thought this could be a good angle to develop a reading challenge for students. I came up with twelve different categories relating to colours and moods and found suggested titles for each category. Sometimes the title of the book or the colour of the book cover decided which category they went into, but more often it was the subject matter of the book that helped me decide.

The beauty of this reading challenge is that it is easy to come up with suggested titles relating to your own stock. And it doesn't have to be limited to fiction, for example The Future's Orange could include books on space travel and gadgetry. Scarlet Fever could include books about medical discoveries or the plague!

Each week for a term I highlighted a couple of different colours with large eyecatching headings and selected books for display. I emphasised that the colours could be read in any order, but that the challenge was to read at least one book from each category.

I collected in the Reading Challenge forms towards the end of term and presented prizes to the students who had read the most books.

Suggested time

Students' free time

Target met?

Encourages reading for pleasure and encourages students to try genres they may not have previously considered.

See also

Book Menus

Book Walls

Mission Possible

Speed Dating

Blind Date Reads

Worksheets

on pages 75 & 76

Speed Dating

by Helen Hinks

Type of activity

Promoting reading

Suggested time

Approx one hour

How it works

This was an activity I tried with my reading group which worked successfully. The idea is to divide into two teams - there should be the same number of people in each team. The more people there are in each team the longer the activity will take. Each team member should have brought in a favourite book that they are willing to talk about. To begin with each member of Team One's job is to 'sell' their book to each member of Team Two. They have two minutes to persuade each person from Team Two that this is the most exciting, fabulous book to read. At the end of two minutes I blow a whistle and each person from Team Two moves on to their next 'date'. Once everyone has been seen, the teams swap over and it's Team Two's turn to 'sell' their book.

Students mark their fellow students' books out of five for desirability. The points are totted up at the end of the dating and a prize is awarded to the student whose book gets the highest rating.

Taking it further

You could use Speed Dating as the basis for a display - displaying book covers and opinions on each book.

Target met?

This is a fun way to get students to broaden their reading horizons and it's interesting to find out what students like to read and how enthusiastic they are. It is also a good exercise in encouraging them to speak persuasively.

See also

Book Menus

Desert Island Books

Read a Rainbow

Blind Date Reads

Around the World in Fiction

Worksheet

on page 77

Blind Date Reads

by Helen Hinks

Type of activity

Promoting Reading

Suggested time

Approximately one hour

How it works

This is a fun activity for book groups. Students get into pairs and question each other using a crib sheet to discover each others' reading preferences. They then have to use the library catalogue and book websites to find a suitable book for their partner to take home and read.

See also

Book Menus

Desert Island Books

Speed Dating

Mission Possible

Book Walls

Around the World in Fiction

Target met?

A lighthearted activity that encourages students to think more widely about their book choices.

Worksheets

on pages 78 & 79

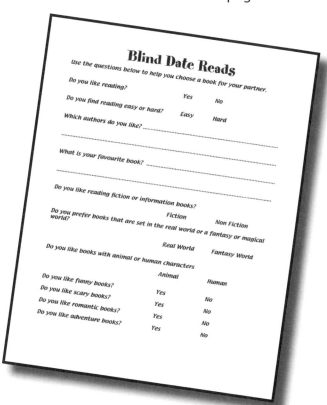

Loyalty Card Scheme

By Sam Emmott

Type of activity

Raising the profile of the Library

Suggested time

For students' free time

How it works

The loyalty scheme allows you to reward any activity of benefit to the library. It encourages students to feel the library belongs to them and that we appreciate all forms of responsible use. A whole range of activities can be rewarded and you can direct these to areas that you really want to promote, such as increasing reading and borrowing, writing book reviews, designing posters, returning books on time etc.

The rewards must be interesting and/or useful to the students. For a list of the rewards we use see page 80. This is the system we use in our library, but the beauty of it is that the tasks and incentives can be shaped to your own library's needs and priorities.

We created colourful loyalty cards which are compact and just the right size and shape to be used as book marks. The title of the scheme is 'Friends of the Library' and there is a blank space for the student's name. When points are gained we stamp them with a shaped ink stamp and when the points are cashed in we cut the stamp out with a shaped cutter. There are only twenty points on each card. If a student wishes to save points up for a larger reward the full cards can be stored safely in the library.

When issuing and removing points we wanted a system that could not easily be forged so we needed a specific stamp and cutter. Finding a small enough stamp was impossible and in the end we cut up an old 'LIBRARY' stamp and stuck it to a new handle to form 'LIB' which is small enough to cover each individual number on the card. A small

shaped cutter/stamper can be found in most craft shops, the downside being they can only cut/stamp out at the edge of the card so this had an impact on the shape of the loyalty card and the position of the numbers on them.

Taking it further

Get school groups such as the School Council and the Parent Friends Association involved. They could help promote the scheme and fund some of the rewards.

See also

Murder in the Library

Guess Who's Coming to Dinner

Best Borrowers

Worksheet on page 80

Create a Learning Climate

By Anne-Marie Tarter

Type of activity

Raising the profile of the library

Suggested time:

Ongoing

How it works

We often run our library/LRC in an environment which started life as something completely different - a couple of classrooms or the old school hall perhaps. Budgets are tight and sometimes it's difficult to create a fantastic environment which welcomes the students and emphasises the importance of learning and reading.

However there is still plenty that can be done cheaply and easily to create a learning climate and to get our message across to students that the library/LRC is a cool place to be.

A taster of ideas
(tried and tested by me in my library!)

Create different activity zones - quiet zones, comfy reading zones, group work - chatty zones, computer zones.

Display pupil artwork and any library based work.

Display 'Got Caught Reading' pictures of school 'personalities' reading!

Offer bookmarks for free on the counter. Make them to go with your displays. Get students to design them with phrases saying what they like best about the library. Make sure you change them frequently so students want to collect them!

Provide games and chess sets. I liaised with the Maths department for ideas.

Have book trolleys with casual piles. Display books facing outwards on the shelf. Look at book shops for ideas and try to do 'un-librarian' things like leaving books in piles where students congregate.

Provide personal stereos. (I know... but it really does keep the noise down. Try it, you might be surprised!)

Have stationery supplies on hand. The goodwill you gain more than pays for paper, glue, staples, scissors, hole punch...

Keep a supply of sweets, tissues and other comforts. (Many a tear has been shed in my office... and faith restored!)

Have an open door policy! (If you don't like people, why are you in the job anyway?!)

Target met?

Encourages students to take ownership of the library and to view it appropriately as a learning and fun environment.

See also

Best Borrowers

Murder in the Library

Guess who's Coming to Dinner

Transition Project

Around the World in Fiction

By Heather Handley

Type of activity

Promoting reading and Quiz/Competition

Suggested time

One hour lesson
or a period of days as a competition

How it works

We have done this activity to tie in with World Book Day. We use an outline map of the world with boxes around the edge pointing to particular countries/regions. I put on display a selection of fiction books matching those countries. Students have to look at the title, cover or blurb to work out where the story is set and then write the title in the correct box.

There are usually several possibilities for each one plus a couple of 'joker' books such as 'Around the World in Eighty Days' and 'Folk Tales from Around the World' which can be used once only for any box if they get stuck. I put out atlases to help and students work in groups and really enjoy competing with each other to finish first. They all learn some geography and discover fiction books that they may not otherwise look at.

An outline Peters Projection World Map can be downloaded from the Carel Press website and a range of alternative world maps can also be purchased.

Taking it further

I've used this in Year 7 English lessons to tie in with World Book Day, but it could work equally well as a competition for individuals or groups of students. You could also turn it into a display following the competition, with a large map of the world and book covers on display pointing to the appropriate country.

Target met?

Encourages students to read more widely and to be aware of books and authors they may not previously have considered.

See also

Desert Island Books

Book Walls

Book Menus

Speed Dating

Primary to Secondary Transition Project

by Marion Milroy

Type of activity

Raising the profile of the Library *and* Getting to Know the Library

Suggested time

One hour lesson
Approx one hour preparation needed

How it works

I took about a dozen photos of library oriented objects and pursuits - a trolley of books, me at the counter, the magazines and periodicals, a couple of students studying etc. I printed them off so that I had two copies of each. When the Year 6s came in for their transition lesson they were each given a card and had to find their identical 'twin'. This became the person they sat with and worked with. When giving the photos out I tried to keep track of pupils' different coloured jumpers to make sure that they ended up with someone they didn't know!

They sat in their pairs and we brainstormed why the library/LRC is important, who would use one, where you would find one and what sort of things you would use it for. They were expected to make notes (page 81) as an aide memoir and then turn their notes into a mind map (page 82) using words or pictures depending on their skills and abilities. Each part of the session allowed each child to think, write, or be creative depending on their strengths.

Taking it further

You could make a display of the mind maps and have it ready for September to welcome the Year 7s and to serve as a reminder of the work they did while they were still at primary school.

Target met?

A useful way to introduce primary school pupils to their library and to help them feel more familiar when they start secondary school in September.

See also

Create a Learning Climate

Murder in the Library

The Dewey Game

Non Fiction Detective

Worksheets

on pages 81 & 82

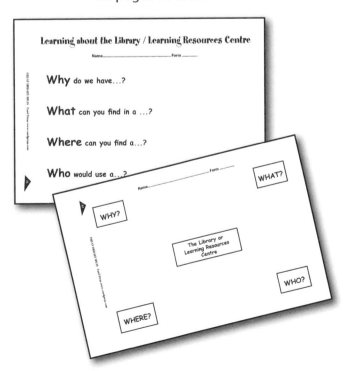

Dewey Jumble Sale
by Jenny Dening

Type of activity

Getting to Know the Library

Suggested time

One hour lesson
5 minutes preparation

How it works

This works well as an activity for Year 7 induction and could also be used as a primary transition lesson.

Before the lesson the librarian selects three resources (if 30 students in a class) from each Dewey hundred and puts them on the table in a jumble. Allocate each pupil a 'Dewey hundred' by going around the class 000; 100; 200 .....900 etc. Thus you should end up with two or three pupils with the same Dewey hundred. Make sure they see who the others in their Dewey hundred are as they will be working with them. You could always give them labels for their jumpers on which they write down which Dewey hundred they represent.

At this point it is worth doing a quick revision of how non fiction books are organised and the main principles of the Dewey Decimal system.

Every student now looks for a book from the pile which is in their Dewey hundred until there are no books left on the table. Each group goes to the shelves of their hundred and picks out another book and checks the shelves, noting the overall subject content of their Dewey area. The class comes back together to feed back which subjects their Dewey area covers. Ensure each group works out beforehand who is going to say what. Timing is quite critical because it takes up to 30 minutes to feed back in my experience.

Taking it further

This is a good way to introduce the Dewey system and you could always follow it with a quiz such as the Non Fiction Detective, or the Dewey Game.

Target met?

Helps students to understand how the Dewey system is organised and to familiarise themselves with the layout of their own library.

See also

The Dewey Game

Non Fiction Detective

Murder in the Library

Lateral Thinking Game

Library Treasure Hunt Bingo

Book Factor

(We copied the name from X Factor - you could always adapt it to the latest TV show craze!)

by Ann Hannam

Type of activity

Raising the profile of the library

How it works

At least six weeks before World Book Day I invited four members of staff to come to the library during lunch time to read their favourite piece of prose or poetry. As our lunch time is short we only had time for one reader, but this actually worked well as it gave time for feedback and discussion at the end.

Staff members were chosen strategically - one of our staff is an amateur actress and you could always pick the Head of Drama or staff especially popular with the students. On the day, pens and score sheets are distributed to the audience and after each reading, marks are awarded, added up and an average score given. The three judges (could be a mixture of staff and students chosen by you) ask the contestants questions and give a score out of ten which is added to the average score.

During the final the two staff with the highest score could compete against each other to be crowned overall Book Factor winner.

Taking it further

Use your student librarians to help prepare the event - it's good practice for them. Preparation is the key - it can help if you write formally to prospective contestants beforehand (see page 84) and come up with a suitable score sheet. This could be an excellent project for World Book Day events and the final could coincide with World Book Day itself.

Suggested time

Start preparation six weeks beforehand
At least two lunchtimes

Target met?

An excellent way to raise the profile of the library and to give students the opportunity to be involved in planning a special event.

See also

Murder in the Library

Create a Learning Environment

Guess Who's Coming to Dinner

Worksheets

on pages 83 & 84

Stepping Stones

By Rosemary Andrews

Type of activity

Getting to Know the Library *and* Promoting reading

Suggested time

Students' free time over several weeks

How it works

This project is designed to build links between the school library and the local public library and show that the school library does not work in isolation. There are five stages (see worksheet p85) to encourage various skills:

- Reading for pleasure
- Developing information skills
- Evaluating information
- Using a reference library
- Using the internet

As incentives I offer stickers for each step and a small prize when all five steps are completed.

See page 85 for suggested activities, but you could come up with your own depending on the resources in your own library and in the public library.

You need to prepare appropriate lists of books for Steps 1 and 5, and a list of suitable topics for Step 4.

For Step 5 make sure you choose books that are only available from the public library.

Taking it further

Stepping Stones can be used as a springboard for other joint projects. For example, why not ask if you can display student book reviews or other work in the public library?

Target met?

I found this project really useful as a way of building links with the public library and helping students see that the books and information they might need can be available in more than one place.

See also

Desert Island Books

Read a Rainbow

Mission Possible

Worksheet

on page 85

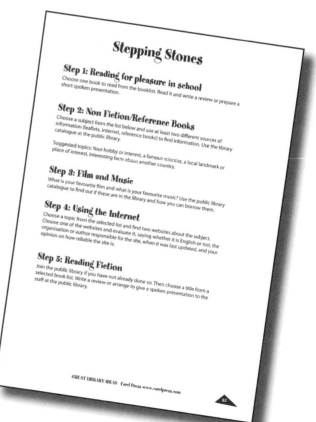

GREAT LIBRARY IDEAS   Carel Press www.carelpress.com

Look for a Book Challenge

By Lesley Cobb

Type of activity

Getting to Know the Library

Suggested time

Time before each lesson to check the shelves
One lesson for the activity

How it works

This is based on the TV game Supermarket Sweep which I play with my Year 7s as part of their Learning to Learn lessons. I use this at the end of a session on the Dewey system, after students have become familiar with the layout of the library and have mastered the art of using the Decoder chart (available from Carel Press), the subject index and looking at the shelf headings.

Students are split into teams of 4 or 5. Each team is given a **different** sheet which has a mixture of questions searching both the fiction and non fiction areas.

Only one student from each team may be out of their seats at any time, although other students in the team can be discussing who is going next and pointing team members in the right direction. Each team member has to find something. Bonus points can be obtained by picking up extra items on the list such as dvds, postcards etc.

An example of the type of quiz sheet I use is on page 86, although you will need to design your own, appropriate to your own stock. If you laminate the sheets they will last longer and save you from printing them out each time.

Check your shelves before you start the game to make sure all the items are there!

Target met?

A fun way to teach the Dewey Decimal system

See also

The Dewey Game

Non fiction Detective

Library Treasure Hunt Bingo

Murder in the Library

The Lateral Thinking Game

Worksheet

on page 86

Look for a Book Challenge

This is a challenge to put to the test what we have talked about today.

You now know how the library is organised and have learnt how to use the CodeCracker charts and the shelf headings.

In your teams you must retrieve the items listed below from the library shelves. You must take it in turns and each team member must have a go.

It is a game of skill against the clock with rewards for the winning team – HOWEVER, only ONE team member may be out of their seats at any time. If you do not follow this rule, points will be deducted!

		Tick when found
1	Find a book from the non fiction shelves about dinosaurs	
2	Choose any title at 914.6 (books about Spain)	
3	Find any Jacqueline Wilson book	
4	Find 'A Christmas Carol' by Charles Dickens	
5	Select Volume 16 of Encyclopaedia Britannica from the Reference Shelves	
6	In the Reference section find the book Essential Articles 10	
7	Find a poetry book which includes some animal poems	
8	Find a book about horses	
9	From the fiction area choose a book by Michael Morpurgo	
10	Find a book about the football World Cup at 796.334	

To earn 4 extra bonus points:

Bring any video with a 12 or PG rating	
Find a German dictionary	

Remember:
Use the Decoder chart or subject index and look at the headings on the shelves. They will help you!

GREAT LIBRARY IDEAS Carel Press www.carelpress.com

101 Reasons to Read a Book

By Lesley Cobb

Type of activity

Promoting reading

Suggested time

Approx two hours preparation
Students' own time over half a term

How it works

This is a really easy book challenge to organise. I usually run it with my Year 7 and 8 students at the beginning of the new school year. I randomly pick out 101 book titles – usually new books that are on display or old favourites from the shelves. I make a list of the books I have chosen which I use to check against the daily issues on the computer.

If a book from the list has been chosen and borrowed, I cross it off the list so that it cannot be re-used. As books are selected, a mini Dalmation picture with the borrower's name and form is stuck up in the library, usually around the new book display. See page 87 for a sample of this.

Students who have selected one of the chosen books are sent a note in their register telling them to come to the library for a reward point. Students often start competing with each other to see who can get the most reward points and thus the most mini Dalmations posted up around the library with their names on.

After all the chosen books have been borrowed, all the names of pupils who have borrowed them are put into a lucky draw for a bigger prize. This reading challenge usually lasts a good half a term. The element of mystery makes it very popular and students look forward to getting a message in their register to tell them to visit the library for their reward point. They also really enjoy seeing the 101 mini Dalmations cropping up around the library with their names on.

Taking it further?

I have a selection of fluffy Dalmation dogs which I have collected from car boot sales to make the display more interesting. You could always encourage students to write book reviews of the books they read to add to the display.

Target met?

An excellent way to raise the profile of the library and promote reading.

See also

Mission Possible

Read a Rainbow

Blind Date Reads

Worksheet

on page 87

Book Menu

Starter

Main Course

Dessert

Name .... Form ....

GREAT LIBRARY IDEAS   Carel Press

✂ --

Book Menu

Starter

Main Course

Dessert

Name .... Form ....

GREAT LIBRARY IDEAS   Carel Press

Desert Island Books!

You are about to be shipwrecked on a desert island. Fortunately the ship you are on has a huge library containing almost every book ever published, so at least you won't be short of things to read!

Your task is to decide on the four books you would most like to have with you on your desert island.

1 ....

2 ....

3 ....

4 ....

From the four listed above, which is your absolute favourite book?

The one book I must have is:

....

Sign/Name ....

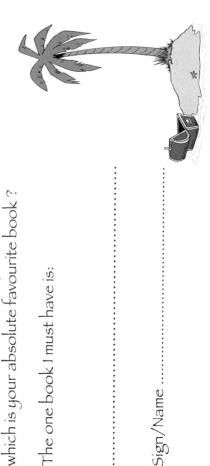

Desert Island Books!

You are about to be shipwrecked on a desert island. Fortunately the ship you are on has a huge library containing almost every book ever published, so at least you won't be short of things to read!

Your task is to decide on the four books you would most like to have with you on your desert island.

1 ....

2 ....

3 ....

4 ....

From the four listed above, which is your absolute favourite book?

The one book I must have is:

....

Sign/Name ....

Send a Text Message to a Book Character!

Choose a character from any book and send him or her a text message.

It could be a character you like, saying why they should hang around with you.

It could be a character you hate, to say what you don't like about him or her.

It could be the main character, the hero or heroine of the book, or a less important character, someone on the sidelines.

It could be a victim, for example someone who gets hurt, telling them not to do or say whatever led them into danger.

Send a Text Message to a Book Character!

Text Message Entry Form

Name .... Form...

1. Set the Scene: explain what has happened in the story so far...

2. Write your message below. (No more than 150 letters!)

3. Explain what effect your message may have on the story.
   Would it have changed the ending?
   Why? Why not?

GREAT LIBRARY IDEAS Carel Press www.carelpress.com

Book Ends Quiz

Name.. Form ....

All these characters are important to each other. Some are in love and others are definitely not! Can you match these book and film pairs?

Q1.   Quiet, studious girl. Likes magic. WLTM Bulgarian Quidditch celebrity with charm and charisma.

ANSWER: ....

Q2.   Above average intelligence 14 year old. Looking for underground fairy for long, intelligent discussions. Must like criminals, gold and technology.

ANSWER: ....

Q3.   Small, sleek, out of this world Hobbit, looking for "Precious" lost partner.

ANSWER: ....

Q4.   Chocolate tycoon seeks willing heir to take up reins. This could be your golden ticket to a shining career.

ANSWER: ....

Q5.   Fit, energetic, sabre wielding male, looking for father from the dark side.

ANSWER: ....

Q6.   Cigarette smoking, curvy, party loving female searching for romantic gentleman to sweep her off her feet.

ANSWER: ....

Q7.   Extra large, ugly, hairy male seeks beautiful princess for love and romance.

ANSWER: ....

Q8.   Count, fallen on hard times, desperately wishes to find lost orphans. Reward guaranteed for information.

ANSWER: ....

Q9.   Italian male of good standing looking for young female for short but sweet romance.

ANSWER: ....

Non Fiction Detective

With your partner can you seek out the following clues?

Name .... Partner ....

We need your help! A thief has broken into the library and stolen some of the books. We need to know whether there are any left for next lesson as a class is coming in to use them!

Can you write down below the DEWEY NUMBER and the TITLE of one book that you can find on the shelves on each of these subjects.

Subject	Dewey No.	Title
Music	....
Volcanoes	....
Cars	....
Computers	....
Victorians	....
Poetry	....

Now: Can you find the following Dewey numbers on the shelves? What are the books at these numbers about?

Dewey No.	Subject
001.942	....
635	....
746	....
822.33	....
937	....
948.02	....

Guess the Genre

Name: .... Form: ....

Can you guess which genre these opening lines are from?
(The genres are all at the bottom of this page)

1) This story begins with a smile ....

2) There is no lake at Camp Green Lake ....

3) In a hole in the ground there lived a Hobbit ....

4) For the two thieves of the 200cc scooter, it was a case of the wrong victim, in the wrong place, on the wrong Sunday morning in September.

....

5) The sheep were released at the Eastern end of the killing pen.

....

6) Paul Faustino slid a blank into the tape recorder and stabbed a couple of buttons.

....

7) It was a funeral in every way but one: the body was missing

....

8) If you are interested in stories with a happy ending, you would be better off reading some other book.

....

More than one book may share the same genre!

Mystery   Animals   Sports

Fantasy   Adventure   Humour   Crime

Find a Fact

Name: .... Form: ....

This is a fun lesson for you. Here's what you have to do:

FIND the multi-volumed reference encyclopaedias

FIND the volume of the Encyclopaedia that begins with the first letter of your surname. (Be very careful here as some of the volumes finish or start with half a letter, for example A-Ch, Ci - G).

LIST anything in that volume that interests you:

....

....

....

READ through the information and
FIND the most amazing fact or sentence you can:

....

....

WRITE it into your own words: and then **ILLUSTRATE** it

....

....

....

....

....

When you have finished put the encyclopaedia volume back in the correct place.   Tick when returned   ✔ ☐

The Shakespeare Reading Game: Shakespeare's Theatre

Name ....   Form ....

The first theatre in London was built in 1567, what was it called?

....

In 1603 Shakespeare's theatre company changed its name to the K...

M.................................... Why? ....

The Globe Theatre was not round. Can you find out how many sides it had? ....

Whereabouts in London was the Globe Theatre? ....

How many people could watch plays in the Globe? ....

Why were some spectators called groundlings? ....

....

How much did it cost to watch a play as a groundling? ....

If you wanted a seat, how much would it cost? ....

Which year did The Globe burn down? ....

Which Shakespeare play was being performed at the time? ....

....

✂ --

The Shakespeare Reading Game: Shakespeare in Stratford

Name ....   Form ....

Shakespeare was born on the .... in the town of

....His father was called .... and his

mother .... His father made his living as a ....

.... William probably started school when he was .... years old.

He went to the local grammar school where the main subjects he learned were ....

and .... In 1582 he married ....

.... They had .... children.

After many years in London Shakespeare returned to Stratford to retire. He bought a large

house called .... He died on ....

aged .... and was buried in .... church in

Stratford. In his will he left most of his property to his daughter ....

but his other daughter, Judith received .... and his wife received the

....

The Shakespeare Reading Game: Shakespeare in London

Name .... Form ....

When did Shakespeare probably go to London? ....

Which group of actors did he join? ....

Find the names of three theatres in London at the time. .... ,

.... and ....

Why did all the theatres have to close down in 1592? ....

When did the theatres reopen? ....

How many people lived in London at that time? ....

Shakespeare worked with many famous actors, can you find the names of three of them?

.... , ... and

....

✂ ---

The Shakespeare Reading Game: Shakespeare's England

Name .... Form ....

Who was queen of England when Shakespeare was born? ....

During the 1580s England was at war with France or Spain (Circle the correct answer)

A large fleet of ships sent to invade England was defeated in 1588. It was called the

S.. A ....

What was the name of the famous English explorer who sailed around the world at this time?

....

Most people lived in the town or the country? (Circle the correct answer).

Write down the names of five things people did for entertainment.

....

....

How did people travel in Shakespeare's time? ....

....

GREAT LIBRARY IDEAS   Carel Press www.carelpress.com

The Shakespeare Reading Game: Shakespeare's Plays

Name ....   Form ....

Shakespeare wrote Histories, Tragedies and Comedies.
Can you find examples of each:

History:

....

Tragedy:

....

Comedy:

....

Choose one play in each group and write down the

Title ....

Where it is set ....

Two of the main characters ....

The year it was probably written ....

Title ....

Where it is set ....

Two of the main characters ....

The year it was probably written ....

Title ....

Where it is set ....

Two of the main characters ....

The year it was probably written ....

The Shakespeare Reading Game: Twelfth Night

Name .... Form ....

Twelfth Night is one of Shakespeare's .... plays. It takes place in the

country of .... and the ruler, or Duke, is called ....

The Duke is in love with a lady called ....who is not in love with him.

A young girl called .... believes she is the only survivor of a shipwreck

and disguises herself as a .... so she can become a page to the Duke. She calls

herself .... She looks very like her brother ....

who is believed lost in the shipwreck.

There are lots of parts in Shakespeare's plays where girls are disguised as boys, but female roles

were always played by .... actors.

The Duke uses his page to send messages to Olivia to try to persuade her to love him. Viola is sad

because she has fallen in love with the Duke.

Living in Olivia's house is her cousin Sir .... , a clown called

.... , her steward .... and her servant girl

.... The others all play a trick on the steward and persuade him that Olivia loves

him. He finds a letter which he is convinced is from Olivia. It tells him to wear ....

.... Olivia is shocked and convinced Malvolio is mad.

Viola's brother ....is discovered to be alive and Olivia, who has

fallen in love with the Duke's page, transfers her love to him. The Duke, who is confused by his

feelings for his page, is delighted to discover she is a girl and marries her.

✂--

The Shakespeare Reading Game:
Find the plays which these everyday phrases come from

Name .... Form ....

The be all and end all ....

A blinking idiot ....

Neither rhyme nor reason ....

Cruel to be kind ....

He hath eaten me out of house and home ....

All that glitters is not gold ....

Too much of a good thing ....

The Dewey Game 000 - 099

Name .... Form ....

**Each Dewey section has 100 whole numbers (for example 200 - 299).
Your Dewey mat will tell you which section you are working in.**

Look at the words and pictures on the mat carefully, can you
guess what some of the books in your Dewey section are about?

....

How many shelves are there in your section? ....

Find the first book in your section. Write down the Dewey number
and the subject of this book:

....

Find the last book in your section. Write down the Dewey number and subject:

....

Find a book about the supernatural. Write down the title and Dewey number.

....

**When you have answered all the questions, each person in the group
should put one foot on the mat and put a hand up.**

The Dewey Game 100 - 199

Name .... Form ....

**Each Dewey section has 100 whole numbers (for example 200 - 299).
Your Dewey mat will tell you which section you are working in.**

Look at the words and pictures on the mat carefully, can you
guess what some of the books in your Dewey section are about?

....

How many shelves are there in your section? ....

Choose a book from the middle of your section. Write down the author,
title and Dewey number of the book.

....

What is the number on the spine of the last book in your section? ....

**When you have answered all the questions, each person in the group
should put one foot on the mat and put a hand up.**

The Dewey Game 200 - 299

Name .... Form ....

Each Dewey section has 100 whole numbers (for example 200 - 299).
Your Dewey mat will tell you which section you are working in.

Look at the words and pictures on the mat carefully, can you
guess what some of the books in your Dewey section are about?

....

Find three books from this section, one from the beginning, one from the middle
and one from the end. Write down the Dewey number and the subject of each one.

....

....

....

Measure the width of the spine of the thickest book. ....

When you have answered all the questions, each person in the group
should put one foot on the mat and put a hand up.

✂ ---

The Dewey Game 300 - 399

Name .... Form ....

Each Dewey section has 100 whole numbers (for example 200 - 299).
Your Dewey mat will tell you which section you are working in.

Look at the words and pictures on the mat carefully, can you
guess what some of the books in your Dewey section are about?

....

How many shelves are there in your section? ....

Find a book with the number 391 on the spine. What is its author and title?

....

Find two books from this section, one from the beginning and one
from the end. Write down the Dewey number and subject of each one.

....

....

When you have answered all the questions, each person in the group
should put one foot on the mat and put a hand up.

The Dewey Game 400 - 499

Name .... Form ....

**Each Dewey section has 100 whole numbers (for example 200 - 299).
Your Dewey mat will tell you which section you are working in.**

Look at the words and pictures on the mat carefully, can you
guess what some of the books in your Dewey section are about?

....

How many shelves are there in your section? ....

Find two books from this section, one from the beginning and one from the end.
Write down the Dewey number and the subject of each one.

....

....

Choose a shelf in your section. **Estimate** how many books there are ....

Now count them! Actual number: ....

**When you have answered all the questions, each person in the group
should put one foot on the mat and put a hand up.**

✂ --

The Dewey Game 500 - 599

**Each Dewey section has 100 whole numbers (for example 200 - 299).
Your Dewey mat will tell you which section you are working in.**

How many shelves are there in your section? ....

Choose a book from your section. Write down the Dewey Number and the Title.

....

Count how many other books have the same Dewey number
as the one above. Number of books at this Dewey number: ....

Find a book about Astronomy. Write down the Dewey number and title:

....

**When you have answered all the questions, each person in the group
should put one foot on the mat and put a hand up.**

The Dewey Game 600 - 699

Name ....   Form ....

Each Dewey section has 100 whole numbers (for example 200 - 299). Your Dewey mat will tell you which section you are working in.

Look at the words and pictures on the mat carefully, can you guess what some of the books in your Dewey section are about?

....

How many shelves are there in your section? ....

Find two books from this section, one from the beginning and one from the end. Write down the Dewey number and subject of each one.

....

....

Record the number of the FIRST book in your section ....

When you have answered all the questions, each person in the group should put one foot on the mat and put a hand up.

✂ --

The Dewey Game 700 - 799

Name ....   Form ....

Each Dewey section has 100 whole numbers (for example 200 - 299). Your Dewey mat will tell you which section you are working in.

Look at the words and pictures on the mat carefully, can you guess what some of the books in your Dewey section are about?

....

Record the number of the First book in your section ....

Double this number ....

How many shelves are there in your section? ....

Find a book about football and write down the Dewey number ....

How many pages are there in this book? ....

When you have answered all the questions, each person in the group should put one foot on the mat and put a hand up.

GREAT LIBRARY IDEAS   Carel Press www.carelpress.com

The Dewey Game 800 - 899

Name .... Form ....

Each Dewey section has 100 whole numbers (for example 200 - 299).
Your Dewey mat will tell you which section you are working in.

Look at the words and pictures on the mat carefully, can you
guess what some of the books in your Dewey section are about?

....

How many shelves are there in this section? ....

Find three books from the section, one from the beginning, one from the middle
and one from the end. Write down the Dewey number and the subject of each one.

....

....

....

Measure the height of the tallest book in your section. ....

When you have answered all the questions, each person in the group
should put one foot on the mat and put a hand up.

✂ ---

The Dewey Game 900 - 999

Name .... Form ....

Each Dewey section has 100 whole numbers (for example 200 - 299).
Your Dewey mat will tell you which section you are working in.

Look at the words and pictures on the mat carefully, can you
guess what some of the books in your Dewey section are about?

....

How many shelves are there in your section? ....

Find a book about Ancient Egypt. What Dewey number is this book? ....

Find the last book in your section and write down the Dewey number: ....

What is the subject of this book? ....

Measure the height and width of this book. ....

When you have answered all the questions, each person in the group
should put one foot on the mat and put a hand up.

Mission Possible
Mission 1

Name .... Form ....

Book Title...

Author ....

Re-read the first two sentences of the book/story. Do you think this was a good opening? Award it marks out of 100 for 'grabability'.

Choose your favourite character. Write down ten words that best describe him or her.

If you were making this book / story into a film, what would you want the audience to see first? Explain briefly how you would start your film.

GREAT LIBRARY IDEAS Carel Press www.carelpress.com

Mission Possible: Mission 2

Name .... Form ....

Book Title ....

Author ....

If you had to spend a day with one character from this book, who would you choose and why? What would you do on your day out?

Which character from your story would you least like to be stuck in a lift with and why?

Where was your story set? Describe briefly what this place was like.

Mission Possible: Mission 3

Name .... Form ....

Book Title ....

Author ....

Would you change any part of the plot? If so, how?

Try to think of a different title for the story.

How did you feel after finishing the book?

GREAT LIBRARY IDEAS Carel Press www.carelpress.com

Mission Possible:
Mission 4

Name .... Form ....

Book Title ....

Author ....

Explain in no more than thirty words what the story is about.

Can you think of at least two questions you could ask the author of this book?

What did you like or dislike about the main character?

Mission Possible:
Mission 5

Name .... Form ....

Book Title..

Author ....

If your book was to be made into a film which film stars would you choose to play the main characters?

Choose your favourite character. Can you think of at least ten words to describe him or her?

Where was your story set? Describe briefly what this place is like.

 GREAT LIBRARY IDEAS Carel Press www.carelpress.com

Mission Possible: Mission 6

Name .... Form ....

Book Title...

Author ....

Out of the six books you have read which was your favourite and why?

Re-read the first two sentences of the book/story. Do you think
this was a good opening? Award it marks out of 10 for 'grabability'.

Explain in no more than 30 words what the story is about.

Mission Possible
Suggested themes for Book Lists

Bronze and Silver Awards:

Award winning authors

Books in diary or letter form (could be fiction and non fiction)

Collections of short stories

Novels from or about another culture

Novels written before 1914

Stories of the supernatural

Future Worlds - stories from fantasy and science fiction

Going for Gold Award:

Books with travel and adventure as a theme

Autobiographies or biographies

Novels by Thomas Hardy or Charles Dickens

Historical novels

Modern classics

GREAT LIBRARY IDEAS   Carel Press www.carelpress.com

Murder in the Library!

A Murder is about to happen in the library
Are you a good enough detective to solve the mystery?

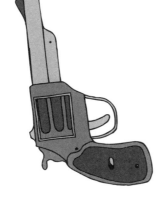

Visit the Library on

···········

And prepare to be SHOCKED!

Murder in the Library!

Murder Most Foul!

A murder is about to be unveiled!!!

Are you a good enough detective
to solve the mystery?

Come to the library on

....

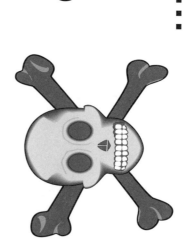

And discover more!

GREAT LIBRARY IDEAS   Carel Press www.carelpress.com

It's MURDER in the library!
WEEK 2 - How the crime was committed!

Name ....   Form ....

Solve the clues below using your library skills.
Then rearrange the FIRST letter ONLY of each answer to spell out the name of the unfortunate victim.

Questions   **Answers**

1. What is the capital city of Canada?   ___ ___ ___ ___ ___ ___

2. Which country has Rome as its capital?   ___ ___ ___ ___ ___

3. Which country has Warsaw as its capital?   ___ ___ ___ ___ ___ ___

4. What is the capital city of Kenya?   ___ ___ ___ ___ ___ ___ ___

5. Which country has London as its capital?   ___ ___ ___ ___ ___ ___ ___

6. What is the capital of Norway?   ___ ___ ___

7. Which country has Copenhagen as its capital? ___ ___ ___ ___ ___ ___ ___

8. Which country has Madrid as its capital?   ___ ___ ___ ___ ___

Now take the FIRST letter of each answer and rearrange them to find out how the victim died.

The Victim died by being   ___ ___ ___ ___ ___ ___ ___ ___

Keep this sheet until next week, then collect the next set of clues from the library to find out who is the murderer

Guess Who's Coming to Dinner - Characters & Props

Winnie the Pooh: Balloon, honey, badly spelt note.

Famous Five: Picnic basket, ginger beer, tin of dog food.

Paddington Bear: Jar of marmalade, luggage label, atlas of Peru.

James Bond: Tube map of London, cigarette case, gun, cocktail shaker.

Goldilocks: Porridge, sugar, bowl and spoon, note saying sorry.

Shhhh.....Who's Been Reading Here? Characters & Props

Dorothy. The Wizard of Oz

Pair of red shoes, books on tornadoes, dog care and map reading and a page open on emeralds.

Paddington Bear

Duffle Coat, an orange and sugar. Books on South America and marmalade making.

Alice Through the Looking Glass

Alice hair band, mirror, clock, white rabbit, books on cats, rabbits and time.
Page open on twins.

Vincent Van Gogh

Book on Holland, yellow paint and brush, ear, picture of sunflowers.

Anne Frank

Diary and pencil, star of David, books on Holland and tulips.

Goldilocks

Porridge bowl, teddy bears, book on DIY.

Scrooge

Treasure chest with chocolate coins, padlock and night cap,
books on celebrating Christmas and relationships.

Harry Potter

Bottle of Butter Beer, round glasses, books on Quidditch and spells.

Library Treasure Hunt Bingo
Suggested Resources to be Found

 A fiction book

 Today's newspapers

 A book about your local area

 An encyclopaedia

 An audio book

 A reference book

 A non fiction book

 Something from your teacher

 A magazine

 A poetry book

The Web versus Books

Name ....

Form ....

Finding the Information

For this activity you will need to work in pairs. Here are a series of seven research scenarios. For each one you need to decide whether it will be quicker, easier and more relevant to use a book to find the information, or the internet.

To start with read each research scenario and jot down next to it which source of information you think will be best. Then have a go at the research and make notes about how easy it was to find the information using your chosen source. Make sure you quote each source. Later we will discuss your findings with the rest of the class.

Research Scenario:	Book or internet?	Notes about research (including source)
What are the opening hours of the Colosseum in Rome?		
In what city would you find the famous Rialto Bridge?		
Which city is further south, Naples or Milan?		
What are the two large islands off the coast of Italy?		
Which year was Pompeii destroyed by Mount Vesuvius?		
Are there any rules to follow when visiting the Vatican?		
How much is a train ticket from Ciampino Airport to Roma Termini?		

Take a Book by its Cover - Lesson Notes

Introduce Topic

This lesson will help us to think about how we choose books and how important book covers are in influencing our choice. To get us thinking we will begin by looking at sweets and how important their packaging is.

Discuss sweets in table groups.

List what makes sweet packets look attractive.

Think about: For whom is the packet designed? (colourful packets and well known characters may attract younger children)

Is it easy to share? Is this preferred?

Is it easy to open?

Is it designed to be consumed in one sitting, or last longer? (Can the packet be closed and reopened easily?)

Does the product live up to the expectations of the packet? How do we find out? (by tasting them!)

Discuss books in table groups. Have plenty of examples available.

Think about: The picture on the front cover

The style of lettering and any strap or shout line

The blurb/synopsis on the back

Any recommendations

Any extra information that the cover gives us

By the end of the lesson students should be able to:

List key elements that make an enticing book cover.

Identify the audience that the book is aimed at

Explain and justify their reasons.

The Lateral Thinking Game

Do not use the library catalogue for this game, instead look around the library and check the **Shelf Headings**.

Work in pairs and discuss with your partner which resources should be included on your list. Check with the library staff if you are unsure whether an answer is allowable.

Think in broad terms and think laterally!

If you have been given a person to look up you could think about:

The way they look

The way they speak

What they eat

What possessions they have

Where they live

What job they do

What they have achieved

What hobbies they have

If you have been given an object to look up you could think about:

What it looks like

What you use it for

Why you use it/Why you need it

What it represents

REMEMBER
to ask the library staff if you need help

GREAT LIBRARY IDEAS   Carel Press www.carelpress.com

Lateral Thinking in the Library

Names .... Form ....

Library Topic: ....

For each area write in the title, author and Dewey number of one resource you have found that is connected to your topic.

Shelf Heading	Title and Author	Dewey No
Fiction		
Audiovisual		
Reference		
Psychology Philosophy Religion		
Media Politics Economics		
Social Science Environment Military		
Mythology Fashion		
Science History Maths Physics Chemistry		
Physical Geography Biology		
Applied Science		

Names .... Form ....

Library Topic: ....

Lateral Thinking in the Library 2

Shelf Heading	Title and Author	Dewey No
Art		
Music		
Sport		
Literature or Classics		
Human Geography		
World History		
British History		
French German Foreign History		

Score extra points if you can....

Use a dictionary to translate your topic word into another language ....

Find a non-book item likely to have information on your topic (write down title)

....

Find a website related to your topic (write address) ....

Reading Challenge

Read a Rainbow

Name ....

Form ....

GREAT LIBRARY IDEAS   Carel Press

Browned Off	Scarlet Fever	Mellow Yellow
Whiter Shade of Pale	Green with Envy	Tickled Pink
Jet Black	Shrinking Violet	Feeling Blue
Future's Orange	Silver Lining	Multi Coloured Swapshop

GREAT LIBRARY IDEAS   Carel Press

Colour	Author	Title

GREAT LIBRARY IDEAS Carel Press

Whatever mood we are in there is often a book that can help. Whether you want some excitement or just a story to help you escape from the hubbub around you.

Books come in lots of different 'colours'. Each week this term the library will highlight different 'colours' - whether it's in the title of the book, the colour on the book cover, or the genre of the story. How many can you read?

You can read the books in any order.

When you have finished a book - record the details in the table in this leaflet and take it to the librarian who will stamp it.

These forms will be collected in during the last week of term and prizes awarded to the students who have read the most books. Go on - read a rainbow!

Colour	Author	Title

GREAT LIBRARY IDEAS Carel Press

Speed Dating

When the whistle blows find a partner and listen while they 'sell' their book to you. When the whistle blows a second time fill in the name of the person who talked to you, the title and author of their book and your score out of 5 for how much you would now like to read the book.

Name .... Form ....

Name	Title	Author	Score

Speed Dating

When the whistle blows find a partner and listen while they 'sell' their book to you. When the whistle blows a second time fill in the name of the person who talked to you, the title and author of their book and your score out of 5 for how much you would now like to read the book.

Name .... Form ....

Name	Title	Author	Score

Blind Date Reads

Name .... Form ....

Use the questions below to help you choose a book for your partner.

Do you like reading?   Yes   No

Do you find reading easy or hard?   *Easy*   *Hard*

Which authors do you like? ....

....

What is your favourite book? ....

....

Do you like reading fiction or information books?

                                             Fiction   *Non Fiction*

Do you prefer books that are set in the real world or a fantasy or magical world?

                                             Real World   *Fantasy World*

Do you like books with animal or human characters

                                             Animal   *Human*

Do you like funny books?   Yes   *No*

Do you like scary books?   Yes   *No*

Do you like romantic books?   Yes   *No*

Do you like adventure books?   Yes   *No*

GREAT LIBRARY IDEAS   Carel Press www.carelpress.com

Blind Date Reads Continued...

Name .... Form ....

Now you have some information about your partner's reading preferences, you need to decide on the best way to find a book for your partner.

Here are some web sites you could use to help you choose a book for your partner:

Cool Reads: www.cool-reads.co.uk

Mrs Mad: www.mrsmad.com

Reading Matters: www.readingmatters.co.uk

You could also use the library catalogue or the subject index to find Dewey numbers. Remember to check that we have copies of the books that you choose.

~~~~~~~~~~~~~~~~~~~~~~~~

Which book did you choose for your partner?

Title: ....

Author: ....

Why did you choose this book? ....

....

Ask your partner to fill in this section when they have read the book you chose for them.

Did you enjoy this book?   *Yes*   *No*

Is it a book you would normally have picked for yourself?

                               Yes   *No*

Do you think your partner made a good choice?

                               Yes   *No*

Loyalty Scheme

Activities	Points Awarded
Write a review of a book that the library holds	10
Write an article for the library magazine	20
Participate in one of the library competitions	5
Request a new and useful resource for the library	1
Quote a library resource in homework	5
Behave well (at librarian's discretion)	1
Supervise the IT room for half an hour (older pupils only, librarian's choice, must make themselves useful)	10
Spend a lot of time in the library (librarian's discretion)	Varies
Tidy away correctly five items	1
Help to tidy the library at end of school, breaks or lunch	5
Design posters or artwork for the library	varies
Attend a library club, society or quiz	2
Achieve something	varies
Read the full set of something	5
Write a critique of an existing review in the review file	2
Carry out research in the library	varies
Teacher's recommendations	varies
Services to the library	varies
Good librarian points, per duty	1

Loyalty Scheme Rewards

1 point	=	1p off fines
1 point	=	1p off photocopying
1 point	=	1p off any stationery item
5 points	=	borrow an extra book or video
10 points	=	a book mark or reward pencil
100 points	=	a pencil case, pocket stapler or correction pen
250 points	=	a book lucky dip, nylon briefcase or PE bag
500 points	=	£5 voucher
1000 points	=	£10 voucher

Learning about the Library / Learning Resources Centre

Name...

Why do we have....?

What can you find in a ....?

Where can you find a....?

Who would use a....?

Name..

WHAT?

WHO?

The Library or
Learning Resources
Centre

WHY?

WHERE?

GREAT LIBRARY IDEAS Carel Press www.carelpress.com

Book Factor!

Dear

We would like you to take part in **Book Factor!** as part of our celebrations for World Book Day. You are invited to visit the library on .... to read your favourite poem, or a piece of prose from your favourite book.

Your reading should take at least ten minutes, but not more than fifteen. The **Book Factor!** judges and audience will judge the quality of your reading and give you a score.

You will be invited back with the other contestants on .... when a panel of judges with give all contestants feedback and scores. This will be followed by a prize giving for the winner and runners up. Light refreshments will also be served.

We do hope that you can join **Book Factor!**
Yours sincerely,

✂ --

Book Factor!

Dear

We would like you to take part in **Book Factor!** as part of our celebrations for World Book Day. You are invited to visit the library on .... to read your favourite poem, or a piece of prose from your favourite book.

Your reading should take at least ten minutes, but not more than fifteen. The **Book Factor!** judges and audience will judge the quality of your reading and give you a score.

You will be invited back with the other contestants on .... when a panel of judges with give all contestants feedback and scores. This will be followed by a prize giving for the winner and runners up. Light refreshments will also be served.

We do hope that you can join **Book Factor!**
Yours sincerely,

Book Factor! Score Sheet for Contestant:

[ ]

Circle a score for each of the following questions. 1 = Poor, 10 = Fantastic

1.   How much effort did they put into their reading?

   Poor **1** **2** **3** **4** **5** **6** **7** **8** **9** **10** **Fantastic**

2.   Do you think they were skilful, for example were they good at reading or did they make lots of mistakes?

   Poor **1** **2** **3** **4** **5** **6** **7** **8** **9** **10** **Fantastic**

3.   Did their voice change for different characters or settings, or did they read in the same voice all the way through?

   Poor **1** **2** **3** **4** **5** **6** **7** **8** **9** **10** **Fantastic**

4.   Did they use their body to help with the reading, eg did they move their arms or shake their head or did they stand still?

   Poor **1** **2** **3** **4** **5** **6** **7** **8** **9** **10** **Fantastic**

5.   Did they use any objects or props to make the reading more interesting?

   Poor **1** **2** **3** **4** **5** **6** **7** **8** **9** **10** **Fantastic**

6.   What did you think about the choice of reading, was it unusual, different, popular or was it something you didn't like?

   Poor **1** **2** **3** **4** **5** **6** **7** **8** **9** **10** **Fantastic**

7.   How long did the reading take, was it within the 15 minutes or was it too long or too short?

   Poor **1** **2** **3** **4** **5** **6** **7** **8** **9** **10** **Fantastic**

8.   How interesting or appealing was the reading to you?

   Poor **1** **2** **3** **4** **5** **6** **7** **8** **9** **10** **Fantastic**

Finally is there a question you would like to ask the contestant?
If so, put your hand up, ask your question and write down the answer below.
Alternatively use this space to add any other comments that we
could use to help judge the contestant.

....

....

Stepping Stones

Step 1: Reading for pleasure in school

Choose one book to read from the booklist. Read it and write a review or prepare a short spoken presentation.

Step 2: Non Fiction/Reference Books

Choose a subject from the list below and use at least two different sources of information (leaflets, internet, reference books) to find information. Use the library catalogue at the public library.

Suggested topics: Your hobby or interest, a famous scientist, a local landmark or place of interest, interesting facts about another country.

Step 3: Film and Music

What is your favourite film and what is your favourite music? Use the public library catalogue to find out if these are in the library and how you can borrow them.

Step 4: Using the Internet

Choose a topic from the selected list and find two websites about the subject. Choose one of the websites and evaluate it, saying whether it is English or not, the organisation or author responsible for the site, when it was last updated, and your opinion on how reliable the site is.

Step 5: Reading Fiction

Join the public library if you have not already done so. Then choose a title from a selected book list. Write a review or arrange to give a spoken presentation to the staff at the public library.

Look for a Book Challenge

This is a challenge to put to the test what we have talked about today.

You now know how the library is organised and have learnt how to use the **CodeCracker** chart and the shelf headings.

In your teams you must retrieve the items listed below from the library shelves. You must take it in turns and each team member must have a go.

It is a game of skill against the clock with rewards for the winning team – **HOWEVER**, only **ONE** team member may be out of their seats at any time. If you do not follow this rule, points will be deducted!

		Tick when found
1	Find a book from the non fiction shelves about dinosaurs	
2	Choose any title at 914.6 (books about Spain)	
3	Find any Jacqueline Wilson book	
4	Find 'A Christmas Carol' by Charles Dickens	
5	Select Volume 16 of Encyclopaedia Britannica from the Reference Shelves	
6	In the Reference section find the book Essential Articles 10	
7	Find a poetry book which includes some animal poems	
8	Find a book about horses	
9	From the fiction area choose a book by Michael Morpurgo	
10	Find a book about the football World Cup at 796.334	

To earn 4 extra bonus points:

	Bring any video with a 12 or PG rating	
	Find a German dictionary	

Remember:

Use the Decoder chart or subject index and look at the headings on the shelves. They will help you!

GREAT LIBRARY IDEAS   Carel Press www.carelpress.com

101 Reasons to Read a Book

Borrow a fiction book from the library and you could win a fabulous prize!

101 mystery books have been randomly chosen.

If you borrow one of the mystery books, you will receive a reward point. Each reward point is worth one Dalmation puppy!

Start a collection of Dalmation Puppies with your name on all around the LRC.
See how many you can collect!

Once all 101 Dalmations have been found, all the lucky winners will have their names entered into a draw for the star prize!

Name ....

Form ....

Name ....

Form ....

Extras!

Why not hold a **library sleepover, or a late night event**? An overnight stay counts as a school trip so there is some paperwork involved, but it's well worth the effort! We ordered pizzas, played games, read ghost stories, watched a film and then settled down in sleeping bags for the night. Great fun for all, and a fantastic ice breaker for new Year 7s.
Stefany Brown

We celebrate **National Poetry Day** by asking staff and students to nominate their favourite poems. I put out plenty of poetry books for inspiration. On the day I paper the library with printouts and photocopies of all the recommended poems, using brightly coloured paper and adding as many illustrative pictures as I can. I try to make it look as though there are poems everywhere! At lunchtime we hold a special event for staff and pupils to read aloud their favourite poems.
Jennifer Toerien

Hold a **Bring and Buy Sale**. Get students to bring 'as new' books from home to sell. We also do face painting and have cakes and biscuits for sale. Before the event, we ask the pupils to write a quiz about books which we sell for a few pennies on the day and prizes are awarded at a later date for the winners. It's a great way to raise funds for charity or for your library.
Stefany Brown